Bowler's
Start-UP

A Beginner's Guide to Bowling

 Start-Up Sports

By *Doug Werner*

Start-Up Sports, #5

Tracks Publishing
San Diego, California

794.6
WER

Bowler's Start-Up
A Beginner's Guide to Bowling
By Doug Werner

Published by:
Tracks Publishing
140 Brightwood Ave.
Chula Vista, CA 91910
(619) 476-7125

Publisher's Cataloging in Publication
(Prepared by Quality Books Inc.)

Werner, Doug, 1950-
   Bowler's start-up : a beginner's guide to bowling / Doug Werner.

   p. cm. -- (Start-up sports)
   Includes bibliographical references and index.
   Preassigned LCCN: 95-61506.
   ISBN: 1-884654-05-3.

   1. Bowling.   I. Title.   II. Series.

GV903.W47 1995   794.6
                                    QBI95-20430

Dedicated to
Kathleen Wheeler

Acknowledgments

Ebonite International, Inc.
Bill Scheid
Bill Supper
Judy Garrity
Remo Picchietti, Sr.
American Bowling Congress
Mark Miller
Bowling, Inc.
R Lance Elliott
Bowling Hall of Fame
John Dalzell
Bowlers Depot
Jim Lewis
Joseph V. Caracciolo
Zach Ardagna
Wesley Popplewell
Janice Popplewell
Mike Wilson
Debbie Ayers
Town & Country Lanes
Kearny Mesa Bowl
Ed Pelletier
John Horger
Joel Bautisa
Eugene & Ann Werner
Camera Bug
Lynn's Photo
Jim & Dee Mitten
Billy Bo Button
Lulu La Rue
Chris Reinhard
Rudy Southerland
Shelly Blair
Kensington Type
Tamara Parsons
ColorType

Preface

Bowling is the Great American Recreation. It's woven into the fabric of most of our lives. It's almost pointless to talk numbers because nearly everyone has bowled at one time or another. It's like asking folks if they've ever played catch. Or gone to the movies. Or ridden a bike.

And like catch, or the movies, or bicycle riding, we sometimes take bowling for granted. Not because it's forgettable, but because it's so pervasive. It's everywhere. It's always been around and probably always will be.

That's because bowling is a game for everybody. ***It's a game everybody can get up and do!***

Anyway, enjoy the book. It's designed to be j-u-s-t informative enough to get you going. And entertaining enough for you to finish.

Then get outta here and bowl a few.

Bowl Dog

Contents

Preface —————————————— 5

*Introduction/ **Bowler Nation*** —————— 9

Chapter 1/ **Garb & Gear** —————— 19

Chapter 2/ **The Game** —————— 25

Chapter 3/ **Scoring** —————— 35

Chapter 4/ **Courtesy** —————— 41

Chapter 5/ **Safety** —————— 45

Chapter 6/ **Shadow Bowling** —————— 47

Chapter 7/ **Basic Bowling** —————— 55

Chapter 8/ **What's Your Ball Doing?** ———— 67

Chapter 9/ **Spare None!** —————— 75

Chapter 10/ **Leftys** —————— 81

Chapter 11/ **Final Frame** —————— 83

Chapter 12/ **Bowlers Timeline** —————— 89

Glossary —————————————— 93

Resources —————————————— 97

Bibliography —————————————— 103

Index —————————————— 105

Old time alleys were sorta like saloons. Dark, dank and somewhat suspect. Women were not welcome, but the persistent ones were allowed to bowl behind curtains. *(Photo courtesy of the Bowling Hall of Fame and Museum.)*

They used to call them *bowling alleys.*

That name was officially discarded years ago when the first *bowling centers* were built in the `50s. The *alley* word wouldn't do to describe these shiny new edifices springing up across the land. Bowling wanted to reach out to mid-century America and leave its old time, saloon image behind.

And *centers* did just that. Big time. The gleaming, automated bowling center was the kind of place that really wowed `em all. They attracted millions to the sport. Everybody became a bowler. Bowling became mainstream and a mainstay in American culture.

Today, the best centers are like little Disneylands. Replete with restaurants, lounges, child care, billiard tables, amusement/arcade areas, video game rooms, banquet facilities, even volleyball courts. The marketing people like to call them *bowling-based family recreational centers.*

But whatever the name, it's still the *game* that draws

the crowds. Every town that really is a town has a place to bowl. In this country bowling is something of a rite of passage that doesn't ever end. Because people can bowl from age 3 to 103. It's truly a lifetime sport.

RAINBOWL COALITION

In bowling centers people *play*. Everyone is dressed down and feeling up. It's sorta like a day at the ball park except the entire crowd is *participating* in the game. The air is filled with the sound of crashing pins and a hundred happy voices (well, mostly happy). Because it's alotta fun knocking down the pins with your pals.

And the people! All *kinds* of people. Old ones, young ones, fat ones, skinny ones, male ones, female ones, black ones, white ones, expert ones, novice ones, rich ones, and not-so-rich ones. Lordy! It's like the entire rainbow coalition every night (and day).

Haven't all these bowlers heard? Americans are supposed to be a very fragmented lot these days. Nobody gets along anymore. Don't they read the newspapers? Don't they watch TV? What exactly is going on in these bowling centers? What would Ricky Lake say?

If it's all that harmonious maybe the next World Summit should be held in a center *(Bowling for World Peace)*. Or the next round of Major League Negotiations *(Bowling for Dollars)*. For sure the OJ trial should have moved itself into one *(Bowling for Justice)*.

Ah, but I digress.

The reason everybody bowls (and most everybody does bowl, or, as in your case, wants to) is because it's just plain fun. It's also convenient, inexpensive, and cozy. Everybody is friendly at the center (what's there to be unfriendly about when you're bowling?) and as far as I know, they don't allow boom boxes inside. Or tobacco (anymore) or guns or gang-related activities of any sort.

It's a swell time and a great game for all.

There it is.

The *real* American Pastime. For
over 80 million everyday people.

Do ya think this guy thinks bowling's hip? You betcha!

HEY, BOWLING'S COOL!

It slays me sometimes to see how bowling is framed in the public eye by big league advertisers, movie makers, television, and most of the media in general. Like all bowlers wear funny shirts, sport thick middles, guzzle beer, chain smoke, and bray incoherently.

Sure.

Bowling is a game. Bowling is a sport. Although you can have fun with it right from the start, it takes alotta practice and dedication to really get good. Cartoon characters don't cut it.

And 80 million Americans bowl. *80 million!* Who's to say such a mega chunk of our population is unhip? If that many bowl, it sorta negates that notion in a very big way.

Here's the thing. Sending that spheroid down the lane on a crisp course is a true rush. Watching that ball crash into the pocket and scatter the pins is a moment of triumph and exhilaration. Like hitting a ball on the sweet spot of a bat. Trimming the sails after a well executed tack. Slicing a turn just-so on a pair of skies. Or hitting the lip of a wave on a surfboard.

All these things are athletic feats. No more, and certainly no less. *It's what stirs the blood and makes life exciting right now!*

And *that* is definitely cool.

BOWLER NATION

Eighty million is alotta bowlers. That's more than golf, tennis, softball, surfing, skiing, or most any other recreational activity in the USA. Only walking and camping, of all things, beat out bowling as a freetime pursuit. And heck, they aren't even sports, are they?

BOWLER PLANET

Over 110 million folks bowl worldwide in over 80

countries. The international rules-making body is the *Federation Internationale des Quilleurs.* I believe it's somewhere in France *(France?!)*, or New Jersey.

BOWLER BITS*

- Of that 80 mil, 35% are adult women, 32% are adult men, and 33% are younger folks.
- There are over 6 million *real serious* bowlers who compete in leagues.
- The median age is 27.6 years.
- 43% are either executive/management types or professionals.
- 60% attended college.
- The median household income is $38,400.
- 76% are married.
- 75% own a home.
- Abe Lincoln was America's first celebrity bowler.
- Herbert Hoover was such an avid bowler that he had lanes built in the White House.
- Harry Trumen, Richard Nixon, Jimmy Carter, George Bush, and Bill Clinton are Presidents who have frequented the *White House Lanes.*
- According to the *Weekly World News (who?)*, Bowlers have an average IQ of 129. Far above that of golfers (97) and tennis players (109) *(what?)*.

So.

People of all ages and genders bowl. A good many are relatively affluent and well educated. At least two made it into the Oval Office. And they're smarter than practically anyone else.

Whoops!

There goes the *Fred Flintstone Stereotype.*

Sources: Market Facts, Inc., 1993, U.S. Department of Commerce, Bureau Of The Census, Statistical Abstract Of The United States: 1993, American Bowling Congress, 1993, Women's International Bowling Congress, 1993, Young American Bowling Alliance, 1993

The next time you hear
or read about bowling
stereotypes, remember
these gentleman.

(Clockwise) **Sir Francis Drake** held up one of the
most important battles in history to finish his game of
bowls... **Abe Lincoln** was America's first *celebrity
bowler*... **Richard Nixon** and **Bill Clinton** are two
more Chief Executives who have made frequent use of
the *White House Lanes.*

THIS BOOK

This is a how-to guide for *beginners.*

There's more or less two parts to the book. The first part will pretty much get you going. There's some stuff to learn but not so much that you'll fall asleep. We'll get ya geared up, explain things a little, and show you how to roll the ball down the lane.

The second part will be a bit more involved but nothing like doing your taxes or your homework. After all, this is a beginner's book and I do feel obligated to keep it real tame. In the resource section you'll find an excellent source for a number of books and videos that go into the finer points of the game. And believe me there are alot of finer points to this game.

Bowling is sorta like in-line skating or guitar playing. It's pretty easy to pick-up for fun's sake, but you can also take it a long, long way as far as expertise.

Bowling in particular is a very, very precise game and it takes a great deal of concentration and effort to consistently perform well at a higher level. You'll get a glimpse of that later on in the book, but for the most part, *we jus' be havin' fun.*

GET INSTRUCTION

Most bowling centers make it easy to get instruction. Many give lessons free. All the alleys want to cultivate new bowlers.

Nothing can replace quality, real-live coaching. Not the videos, not this book. Some may need it less than others, but it can never hurt and you just may meet the one-of-a-kind instructor who will inspire you.

You'll also meet beginners such as yourself and that ain't bad either. Besides the company, y'all can watch each other and help each other improve.

HANG LOOSE, HAVE FUN

Relax and have fun as you learn. There's something about bowling that almost makes it unnecessary to say that because the sport doesn't have the intimidation factor of, say, snowboarding or sailing. And bowling centers are friendly, family oriented places.

But as you progress, you may become frustrated with your learning curve and the unavoidable slumps. Don't let them get you down! In this sport there are a series of grooves to get into in order to get better. As you bowl (and practice, practice, practice), they'll become more apparent and easier to slide into.

Ready to roll-- Bowling is easy to dress for. Loose and comfy does it. The only special item of apparel is shoes. You must wear bowling shoes when you use the lanes or they will not let you bowl.

Garb&Gear

1

EBONITE

CLOTHING

Bowling is an easy game to dress for. Just **make it loose and comfy. Tight clothing will bind and chafe.**

SHOES

The only other fashion decision involves shoes. **You must wear specially made bowling shoes in order to use the lanes.** They won't let you bowl without them.

No sweat. All bowling centers have shoes for rent. What makes them special are the sliding soles. The toe portions of each are made of soft leather that will allow you to slide when you release the ball.

If and when you decide to buy your own, you can get a pair that has such a sole on one foot and a rubber sole on the other. During the release only one foot does the sliding. The other does the braking. Hence the rubber sole.

It's a good idea to buy your own shoes. Rentals usually fit and look like bozo boots. You can imagine how that'll affect your game. Not to mention your self-image. New shoes aren't expensive and who wants to wear public footwear anyway?

HAVE A BALL

Bowling centers have lots of balls you can use for free. The problem is finding one that:

1) Fits your thumb and the two middle fingers on your throwing hand and...

2) Doesn't weigh too much or too little.

Oh, you'll find a ball that you can use, but chances are it won't be the ideal combination of fit and weight. For that you need to buy your own ball and have it drilled to your exact specs.

House balls are OK for a time or two, but eventually you must get a custom fitted ball in order to move ahead with this bowling stuff. A poor fit will wreck your game. You'll compensate for and concentrate on all the inadequacies of the ball instead of your mechanics. No bueno.

Actually, balls aren't all that expensive and most centers have a pro shop and a person who knows how to measure you for a custom ball.

Meanwhile, search the racks in back of the lanes for a ball that you can comfortably lift, and that you can fit your hand into. Most guys start off with a 14-16 pound ball and ladies a 12-14 pound ball.

The ideal finger/thumb fit is snug enough so that you can j-u-s-t feel the sides of the hole and still pull out easily. When the thumb is inserted all the way into its hole and the fingers are extended over their holes, the second joint should lay about a 1/4 inch beyond the nearest edge of the finger holes.

Conventional Grip-- The fingers insert all the way up to the first knuckles. This is the recommended grip for beginners.

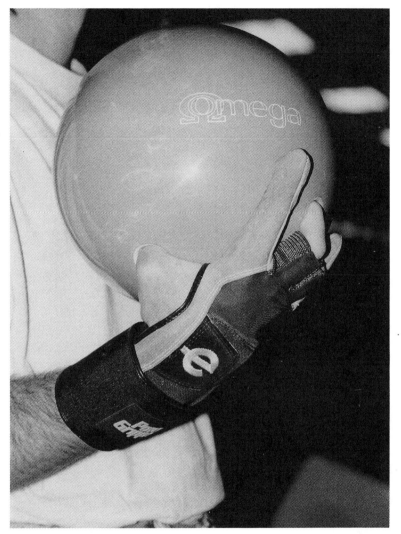

***Wrist Brace*--** Keeps the wrist firm throughout the approach and release.

This will give you what is called a *conventional grip.* Thumb inserts all the way and fingers insert fully to the second knuckle. There are other grips, but the conventional is your best bet right now.

You might get lucky and find a comfy ball right away, and then again, maybe you won't. As you bowl you'll get a better feel for what you need. Try different ones until you're satisfied and then *stick with it.*

The weight is something you'll get used to soon enough. Bowling balls are rather heavy things and should be. After all, they're made to roll and knock down pins. Not to toss, even though a few of you will try. **Find a hefty ball you can control for three or more games.** If it's too light you'll be sending it into the pins too fast and that, believe it or not, is not good. Obviously, if you're struggling with control and your bowling arm is tearing loose, get a lighter ball.

OTHER STUFF

You really don't need anything else other than the shoes and the ball. You'll see other bowlers wearing wrist braces and using other paraphernalia, but don't worry about that for now.

Towels are a good idea, however. One to clean the ball every now and then, and one for your face if you sweat. The lanes are *dressed,* or oiled, on a regular basis and your ball will get a little greasy. Just try to remember which towel wiped what.

RUBY

There was a time when bowling balls came in just one color: black.

No more.

Now they come in every color and pattern imaginable. Heck, they even have balls that glow in the dark.

And so it goes with bowler fashion.

You can still spot folks wearing the frumpy frocks of old, but more likely you'll see a circus of variety at the lanes. Everything from preppie to grunge. Just like at the mall.

But I still remember Ruby.

While waiting to get my ball drilled at a pro shop one day, the young man behind the counter was busy putting the finishing touches on a very bright, red ball. It stood out even there, in a place full of jazzy, colored models.

And then Ruby walked in. Dressed to the nines in ruby red shorts, ruby red blouse, and ruby red shoes. Her hair was a major league monument of whiteness with a tint of violet.

"What's up, Ruby?," greeted the young man as he handed her the ball.

She dipped her ruby red nails into her freshly drilled ball. "That'll do it, hon," she proclaimed shortly. "Just in time for my game."

Then she placed the ball in a ruby red bag, paid the man, and left.

Although I was somewhat stunned by all that redness and all that hair, the rest of the crew in the shop didn't bat an eye. Ruby must have been a regular.

Later on I watched her bowl a few frames. She owned a wicked hook and got three strikes in a row. Man, the dragon lady could bowl!

So never think your new-found sport lacks for sass. Or doesn't allow for personal style. Bowlers can be a pretty wild bunch.

Just remember Ruby.

the Game 2

Bowling is a game of precision. That's the way it's set up and the way it's played. However, there are variables to contend with and there's plenty of room for personal style.

WE GOT SPECS!

There are a ton of specifications concerning the ball, the pins and the lanes in order to keep the sport consistent from location to location. **The *American Bowling Congress* and the *Women's International Bowling Congress* conduct annual certifications at bowling centers to assure their members of standard playing conditions.**

Balls are made of either hard rubber or plastic and cannot weigh more than 16 pounds. They are 27 inches in circumference and about 8 1/2 inches in diameter.

Lanes are made of either wood or a synthetic material and must be level to within 40/1000 of an inch.

Each lane is comprised of exactly 39 identical boards running lengthwise. Each board is a tad wider than an inch. There's an approach area that runs 15 feet to a foul line, and an alley that reaches 60 feet beyond that to the pins. There are guide dots on the approach, at the foul line, and out on the alley next to the spotting arrows. Both dots and arrows are marked in exact locations.

Pins are perfectly placed and racked in triangle shapes of 10 at the far end of the lane. Each pin is 15 inches high. They are made of plastic-coated maple or synthetic material. Pins are 2 inches wide at the base and 4 3/4 inches thick at their widest point, which is 4 1/2 inches above the base. Wood pins must weigh between 3 pounds, 6 ounces and 3 pounds, 10 ounces. Synthetic pins must weigh between 3 pounds, 6 ounces and 3 pounds, 8 ounces.

There's more, but you get the idea. *(Whew!)*

VARIABLES

So all bowling centers are pretty much standardized. When you visit your sister in Tallahassee and you decide to bowl a few, you're not going to discover that Floridians use 35 foot lanes and lead-weighted pins.

However, you will discover significant differences in the way lanes are maintained from center to center. The dressing or oil that is applied daily is applied according to the whim of the proprietor, and that affects how your ball is gonna roll. Some are slicker than others and prevent the rolling ball from interacting with the surface of the lane.

If you develop a hooking ball, for example, the action of your hook will not work on a real slippery lane. A combination of wet and dry spots will further affect the action of your ball. This is when adjustments have to be made, but we're getting ahead of ourselves here.

JUST BOWL `EM OVER

A game of bowling consists of ten *frames*. In each

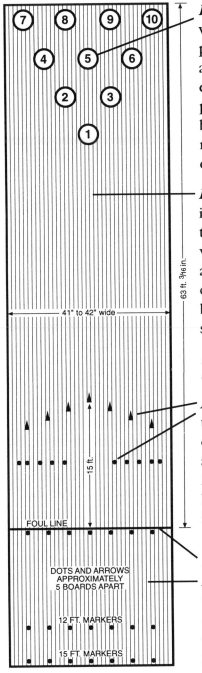

Pins-- In this bird's eye view of a bowling lane, the pins are arranged in a triangular shape at the far end of the alley. Each pin is precisely placed and numbered. This is the way the rack of pins is usually depicted.

Boards-- The lane or alley is comprised of 39 identical boards each a bit wider than an inch. They are precisely positioned in order to provide the bowler with a way to measure ball placement.

Note-- The lane shown is not drawn to proportion.

Arrows and Dots-- No, they are not just pretty designs in wood. The arrows are especially important in aiming the ball. (Make that critically important.)

Foul Line and Approach Area-- This is where you throw the ball from. The dots help the bowler to establish a starting point for each shot.

27

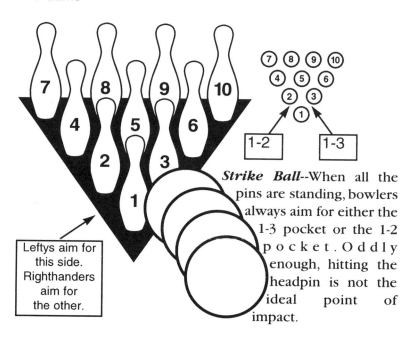

1-2 **1-3**

Strike Ball--When all the pins are standing, bowlers always aim for either the 1-3 pocket or the 1-2 pocket. Oddly enough, hitting the headpin is not the ideal point of impact.

Leftys aim for this side. Righthanders aim for the other.

Strike!-- When the ball is properly placed in the 1-3 or 1-2 pocket, the pins come tumbling down!

frame, each bowler gets two tries to knock down a rack of ten pins. Unless the bowler knocks down all the pins in one or two tries in the tenth frame. Then the bowler gets bonus points. Bowlers earn points in a cumulative fashion that is slightly more convoluted than simply awarding a point-a-pin, yet less complex than nuclear science. We'll cover scoring in the next chapter.

The idea is to knock down as many pins as you can with your ball without scooting over the foul line. Knocking `em all down in one try, each and every turn, is the ultimate goal. Each time you do knock down all ten pins in one try, it's called a *strike*. If you leave some standing after your first roll, but knock them down on your second turn, it's called a *spare*. That's it.

ROCKET THE POCKET!

You don't get a strike (usually) by hitting the pins squarely in the middle of the rack. **The scientifically (literally) proven way to get a strike is to hit the pocket between the headpin (#1 pin) and the next pin over, either right (#3 pin) or left (#2 pin).**

As a rule, righthanders aim for the 1-3 pocket, and lefthanders aim for the 1-2 pocket. Slamming the pocket is the supreme sweet spot in bowling. Developing and maintaining your strike shot is a bowler's lifelong quest and addiction.

SWIFT SPORT

Bowling, by and large, is a brisk game. It moves right along even when several people are playing. As a rule, bowlers pick up their ball when it's their turn and fire away. **Slackers aren't suffered for long.**

I think that because of its speedy nature, bowling doesn't allow the lingering over performance that plagues other sports. There's always another turn coming up shortly and then another game to redeem yourself, if need be.

FLOW ZONE

Bowling is like a dance or an athletic feat that requires the performer to combine total concentration with rhythm and flow. When you're doing it right, you're in a zone where you repeat the winning performance over and over again. It sounds boring, I know, but it isn't. Nothing about being in a zone is.

When you're really with it, it's like that 60 feet between you and the pins doesn't exist. There's an absolute connection between your mind and the pocket. And watching all those pins fall never gets old.

Not that you should expect to get into a zone right away and stay there for long, but *glimpses* of what it's like are readily attainable as soon as you start. Like the feel of a good delivery.

It'll come and go, especially in the beginning, but remember, it's there within each of us to bring out.

YOU GOTTA BELIEVE!

It's funny how one instantly forgets the countless fumbling attempts at attaining a new skill when one finally gets it right.

I thought I'd never throw a hook. That's when the ball sharply breaks into the pins after rolling straight for 30 to 40 feet down the lane. It's the shot used by most top-level bowlers because its angle and spin into the rack is the most effective ball for getting strikes.

It's all in the release. The way the fingers lift and leave the ball at the last second. And I just couldn't get it.

Then it finally happened.

The ball left my hand straight and true, then it swooped into the pins with an unmistakable hooking action. Now it wasn't one of those wild and slashing hooks that you see on TV, but it at least curved. And I was stoked!

Of course, I still couldn't do it every time, but it was

there (somewhere) in me to execute when the stars were lined up correctly. I just had to bring it out. Through concentration and practice. But the hardest part was over.

I knew I could do it.

1 2 3→

***Form and Grace*--** Bowling is so much more than tossing a heavy ball down the lane. To really develop, you must strive for rhythm and consistency, like any athlete or dancer.

***Your Playing Field*--** Dots, arrows, and pins. The arrows will become very important to your game. Especially the second arrow from the right if you're a righthander. Note the long skinny boards that make up the lane. Eventually you'll line-up and adjust your shots using individual board widths as a guide.

***Dressing the Lane*--** Lanes are conditioned with a special dressing that gives each lane its own personality. Understanding and adjusting to the conditions of a given lane will be part of your development as a bowler. The dressing also makes the alley very slippery and hazardous to step on.

***Consoles and Monitors*--** The modern bowling center makes scoring easy. No more pencils or paper! Some systems even tell you where to throw the ball in order to make a spare. Learning how to use these things is only slightly more difficult than dealing with an ATM.

Scoring

Chances are you'll never have to pick up a pencil and score a game. Most centers now have automatic scorers that are very simple to operate. However, it's a good idea to know what's being done for you.

KEEPING IT SIMPLE

So there are ten frames per game during which each bowler gets two tries to knock down the ten pins, except for the last, or tenth frame, in which the bowler may be awarded a bonus turn or turns.

If the bowler never knocks all the pins down during each of his two turns for ten frames, that bowler's score is simply adding a point for each pin knocked down.

As the bowler improves, and begins to knock all the pins down during a single frame, then the scoring starts to get fancy.

If the bowler gets a strike during a given frame, the bowler gets ten points plus the total pinfall from the next *two deliveries*. If the bowler knocks down all the pins in two tries during a frame, this is called a spare and the bowler gets ten points plus the pinfall of the next *single delivery.*

If the bowler gets a strike in the tenth frame, the bowler gets two bonus balls. If the bowler gets a spare, a single bonus ball is awarded.

The highest score a bowler can get is 300. It's called a *perfect game* for good reason. The bowler has tossed nothing but strikes.

SCORING A SAMPLE GAME

You are warned: This is real boring stuff to read!

Each bowler has their game scored in a ten-frame, horizontal grid. Each frame is represented by a box with two smaller boxes inset in the northeast corner, except for the tenth frame box, which has three small boxes inset.

In the smaller boxes go the results of each throw. In the larger boxes goes the cumulative score.

Use an X for a *strike.*

Use a diagonal line for a *spare.*

Use a horizontal line for a *miss.*

0 Use a zero for a *split.* A split is a combination of pins left standing after the first delivery with a pin down immediately ahead of or between them. The headpin must be down as well.

0̸ Use a diagonal line through a zero for a *converted split.* That's a split that's been knocked down.

F Use an F for a *foul.* That's sliding over the foul line during a shot.

Billy	8⊢	⊠	9⧸	7 0							
	8	28	45	52							

Just for Practice

Here we go, frame by frame in an imaginary game:

◄—*Frame #1*-- Your first ball knocks down 8 pins. Put an 8 in the first small box in the upper right corner. Your second throw misses all the pins. Put a horizontal line for a miss in the second box. Put an 8 in the first frame box.

◄—*Frame #2*-- Your first ball is a strike. Put an X in the first small box and leave the big box blank for now.

◄—*Frame #3*-- Your first ball knocks down 9 pins. Put a 9 in the first small box. Your next ball knocks down the remaining pin. This is a spare. Put a diagonal line for a spare in the second box. Don't score in the big box yet.

Now add up the totals of the two throws after your strike with the 10 pins from your strike, and add it all to your first score. That's 10 (for the spare), plus 10 (for the strike), plus 8. Which equals 28. Put 28 in the second frame box.

◄—*Frame #4*-- Your first ball knocks down 7 pins. Put a 7 in the first small box. Now go back to the third frame. Add the 7 pins from your first throw (after the spare) to the 10 pins you scored from the spare itself, and add it to the total in the second frame. That's 7, plus 10, plus 28, which equals 45. Put 45 in the third frame box.

On your second throw you miss the remaining 3 pins which happen to be in a split. Put a zero for a missed split in the second small

Billy	[8]┤	X	[9]/	[7][0]	X	[9]/	[8]/	[7]┤				
	8	28	45	52	72	90	107	114				

box in the fourth frame. Add 7 pins to the cumulative score in the third frame. That's 7 plus 45, which equals 52. Put 52 in the fourth frame box.

◄—Frame #5-- You throw another strike. Put an X in the first small box and move on to the sixth frame.

◄—Frame #6-- You get 9 pins on your first throw. Put a 9 in the first small box. You knock down the last pin with your second toss to get a spare. Put the spare mark in the second small box. Add the 10 pins from the spare, to the 10 pins from the strike, to the cumulative score in the fourth frame, to get the new score for the fifth frame. That's 10, plus 10, plus 52. Which equals 72. Put 72 in the fifth frame box. Leave the sixth frame blank for now.

◄—Frame #7-- You get 8 pins with your first ball. Put 8 in the small box. Now add those 8 pins to the 10 pins from your spare to the cumulative score in the fifth frame. That's 8, plus 10, plus 72. Which equals 90. Put 90 in the sixth frame box.

On your second throw you make a spare by knocking down the remaining 2 pins, which happened to be a split. Put a diagonal line through a zero to indicate a converted split. Since you spared, leave the seventh frame box blank for now.

◄—Frame #8-- You get 7 pins with your first ball. Put a 7 in the small box. Add 7 pins to the 10 pins from the spare, and add them to the score in the sixth frame. That's 7, plus 10, plus 90. Which equals 107. Put 107 in the seventh

Billy	8⊟	⊠	9⧄	7⎸0	⊠	9⧄	8⧄	7⊟	⊠	⊠9⧄	163
	8	28	45	52	72	90	107	114	143	163	

frame box. On your second throw you miss the pins. Put a horizontal line in the second small box. Add 7 pins to your score. That's 7 plus 107, or 114. Put 114 in the eighth frame box.

⊠

143

◄—*Frame #9*-- Strike! Put an X in the first small box and move on to the tenth frame.

⊠9⧄

163

◄—*Frame #10*-- Another strike! You get two more shots. Put an X in the first small box. On your next throw you knock down 9 pins. Put a 9 in the second small box.

Time to add up the score for the ninth frame. That's 10 pins for the strike, plus 9 pins, plus 10 pins for the ninth frame strike, plus the score in the eighth frame. That's 143 points. Put 143 in the ninth frame.

On your third throw in the tenth frame you knock down the last pin for a spare. Put a diagonal line in the last small box. Add up your tenth frame score by adding 10 pins for the spare, 10 pins for the strike, and the cumulative score in the ninth frame. That's 10, plus 10, plus 143, or 163. Put 163 in the last frame. This is your final score.

Lofting-- This is easily one of the most annoying and mind numbing experiences in bowling. Crashing bowling balls are like bombs exploding. Don't *pitch* the ball, *bowl* it!

Bowling centers can be very crowded, busy places. With all the traffic it makes sense that there are some rules of the road. Keep in mind that alotta this stuff boils down to common sense and good sportsmanship.

Here's a compilation of 20 pointers in no particular order:

-- ***Don't loft the ball***-- Bowling ain't throwing. Lofting dents the lane and loosens dentures. Learn the bowling fundamentals and get a ball that fits your hand. Then you will not loft.

-- ***Don't roll your second ball until the first has returned***-- You don't wanna confuse or wreck the machinery. (Can you imagine being a pinboy back in 1932?)

-- ***Don't use another person's ball without their permission***-- This is irritating to the owner and slows down play.

-- ***Keep your personal belongings off the seats and out of the traffic areas***-- Players need to sit and move about freely.

***Don't Wander*--** Stay within your lane.

***Right-of-way*--** Be aware of your neighbors. If they are set-up before you are, let them bowl first.

Chapter Four

-- *Be ready when it's your turn to bowl*-- Keep up with the tempo of the game!

-- *Be quiet in and around your settee area*-- Loud, sharp noises disturb play.

-- *Don't kick the ball return*-- Don't be a crybaby!

-- *Control yourself*-- Don't be a crybaby!

-- *Don't heckle*-- You're not at a political rally.

-- *Don't give unsolicited advice*-- Usually further confuses a slumping bowler.

-- *Don't waste time on your approach*-- Again, remember the tempo of the game.

-- *Don't go onto the approach until it is your turn*-- May cause traffic tie-ups.

-- *Do not stand next to the ball return waiting for your second ball*-- May bother a bowler setting-up next to you.

-- *Stay within your lane*-- Don't dance into another game.

-- *Do not linger at the foul line after delivering the ball*-- Tempo!

-- *Do not carry food or beverages into the approach*-- One spill and everything stops.

-- *Yield to the bowler on your immediate left or right if they are ready to bowl*-- Keeps bowlers from spooking one another.

-- *Spare shooter has right-of-way over bowler with full rack*-- Spare shooters need the courtesy of contemplation.

-- *Show enthusiasm for the game and the efforts of other bowlers!*-- Bowling is a social sport. So be sociable. Give a little and you'll get some back. This promotes good will and insures that everyone will have a good time.

Well *most* everybody, anyway.

Bowling is a bit gentler than alligator wrestling, but there are some things to take note of:

-- ***Keep the approach area free of everything*** -- This is your runway.

-- ***Don't apply powder to help you slide*** -- The stuff will cause someone else to slip.

-- ***Don't step beyond the foul line*** -- The lane is very slick from the dressing. If you don't fall on your butt, you'll track the junk into the approach and cause someone else to slip.

-- ***Don't bowl in street shoes*** -- Leaves smudges in the approach that'll trip everyone up.

-- ***Check the soles of your shoes for foreign substances*** -- You don't wanna track any Bazooka into the approach.

-- ***Take care when picking up your ball from the ball return tray*** -- Don't place your hands and fingers in-between balls.

More Safety Tips:

- Never store your ball in an overhead compartment.
- *Never carry your ball in a shopping bag.*
- Never transport an unbagged ball in the front seat or backseat or trunk of your car.
- *Never practice at crowded playgrounds.*
- Never practice on busy streets.
- *Never stick your head in the ball return.*
- Throw your ball in designated areas only.
- *Never dribble your ball.*
- In a loud voice always shout "Heads Up!" before tossing a ball to anyone.
- *Never plug the finger/thumb holes on another bowler's ball with a foreign substance.*
- Never play *Slip n' Slide* on the lanes.
- *Never bowl angry.*

Avoid smashed fingers-- Pick your ball up from the tray as shown. Do not place hands in-between balls, or yank your ball up with just your fingers in the holes.

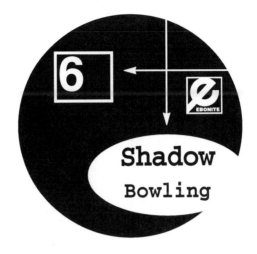

6

Shadow
Bowling

DO YOU TANGO?

Before you head out to the center and try flinging it for real, it's a great idea to try the flinging *without* the ball.

Practicing your bowling moves without the ball is called *shadow bowling*. It's exactly like rehearsing a dance step. Except it's a heck of alot easier!

In the privacy of your home, or backyard, or anywhere, you can go through the motions without worrying about the weight of the ball, the pins you've missed, the guy who wants to bowl behind you, or the nine-year-old in the next lane making it look easy.

Don't worry. I know you're itching to bowl. This won't take alotta time and it really does work. **It'll help you to establish the proper mechanics and rhythm right off. If you take this shadow bowling seriously, then it's just a matter of adding on to the foundation.**

47

FOUR-STEP BOOGIE

Stance--This is also called setting-up. Stand erect with your feet a few inches apart. Place your left foot a few inches in front of your right. (If you're lefthanded, reverse those instructions. And continue to do so as need be.) Pretend you're holding a ball with your right hand and steadying it with your left. Line up the pretend ball in front of your right shoulder about chest high. Your elbow is tucked in. You're loose and relaxed. Knees are slightly bent.

You're ready for the music.

First Step-- This is the most important step. (Again!) **This is the most important step. If you start properly, you'll end-up properly. If you concentrate on this step, the rest just sorta flows.**

Push the pretend ball forward and slightly down, straight out from your shoulder. At the same time move your right foot forward. Move right arm, move right foot.

Second step-- Let the right arm swing down, close to your side, and move your left foot forward. Swing your left arm away from its steadying position on your right to a balancing position on your left.

Third step-- Let the right arm continue its swing back to a point about shoulder level. As you make your third step with your right foot, the arc of your swing has reached its apex.

Fourth step-- The fourth step is the sliding step of your left foot. At the same time your right arm swings back down and forward from the apex of its backswing. **Your timing is correct if your sliding left foot and your swinging right hand come forward simultaneously.**

Follow-through-- Simply allow your swinging arm to continue its course upward.

There it is.

Shadow Bowling (below, left to right)-- It's a good idea to practice the four-step without the ball at first. *Although these pix were shot in a bowling center, you can practice shadow bowling anywhere.*

Set-Up... ***First Step...*** ***Second Step...***

From the set-up, move the ball and your right foot at the same time. This first step establishes the rhythm and flow of your entire approach. Get this much down and you're on your way!

Third Step... ***Fourth Step...*** ***Follow-Through***

You're doin' it right when your throwing arm and your sliding foot arrive together at the finish. The throwing arm draws up and through the target after the ball has been released.

More Shadow Bowling (below, left to right)-- These pix show the same four-step approach from another angle. At this point it's like memorizing a dance step.

Set-Up... *First Step...* *Second Step...*

Note how Wesley sets-up in front of his throwing shoulder and pushes out directly towards his target.

Third step... *Fourth step...* *Follow-Through*

Wesley's non-throwing arm is outstretched to counter-balance the action of his right side. Each step he takes during the approach points straight towards the target.

And More Shadow Bowling (below, left to right) -- The same steps from the rear. *The point of all this shadow bowling stuff is to get you familiar enough with the steps so that when you finally get a ball in your hands, you're not thinking about your feet!*

Set-Up...   ***First Step...***   ***Second Step...***

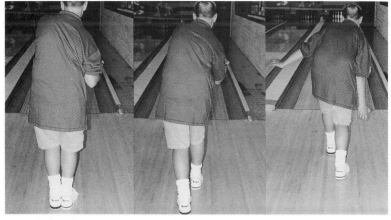

Watch the throwing arm. The ball is pushed *straight* out towards the target... drops *straight* down and...

Third step...   ***Fourth step...***   ***Follow-Through***

... swings *straight* back. It then swings *straight* forward and *straight* up through the target during the follow-through. The arm always swings at a right angle to the shoulders. This is also a good view of Wesley's left arm extension.

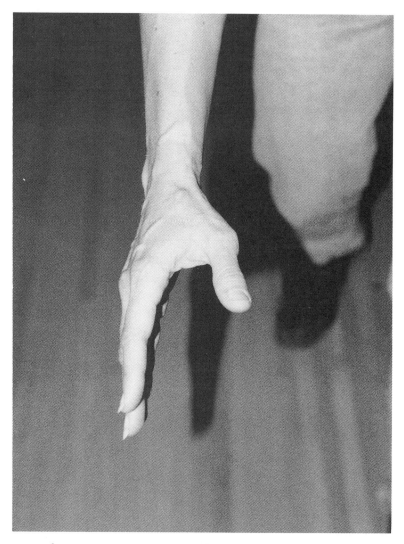

Hand Position-- Howdy! When the ball is released, your hand should be in a handshake mode. Like you're tossing a suitcase. For a righthander, the thumb is in a ten o'clock position.

You have just been introduced to the most basic, and the most recommended approach in bowling. *The four-step approach.* Get it down. Everything else sorta hangs on it.

No, it's not the only way to deliver the ball, however, it is the most fundamentally sound. So at least give it a try. You can always experiment later with other styles.

Rehearse the steps until they become a sweeping, flowing movement. Concentrate on the first step. Move right arm, move right foot. You've got it when left foot and right arm finish together.

Note the swing of your arm. Like a pendulum close to your side. It should swing back and forth at a right angle to your squared shoulders.

HAND POSITION

Just one more thing.

As you shadow bowl, pretend your right hand is carrying a suitcase. **As you follow-through and bring the right arm up and through, your hand should be in a handshake position.** Not palm up or palm down.

REHEARSE

If you can memorize just this stuff, you'll be that much better prepared when you first start chucking the ball down the lane. You can begin to concentrate on other things.

So put on some music and, uh... shake it.

FROM THE SHADOWS

One of the greatest bowlers of all time was probably the greatest shadow bowler that ever lived as well.

Earl Anthony is a member of the *American Bowling Congress* Hall of Fame. He's been Bowler of the Year four times, and has earned more victories in professional bowling than any other bowler in history.

But back when he first became interested in the game, he couldn't afford to pay for all the hours of actual lane time necessary to improve his game. So instead of bowling with a ball, he went through the motions without one. He made arrangements with the alley owner and shadow bowled on any lane that might be empty.

In his book, *Winning Bowling*, Anthony says, "I would sometimes shadow bowl 25 to 30 games a day. It was much less expensive, of course, and it really proved to be most effective in improving my bowling style.

"My bowling started to improve dramatically. In one year, my average had gone into the middle 180s, and in one more year, it was in the low 200s."

I would say that the young Mr. Anthony was one serious dude.

To bowl 25 to 30 *imaginary* games (that's 250 to 300 frames!) must have taken a *massive* level of brute determination and concentration. No ball, no crashing pins, no score, no company. Only the squeaks from his bowling shoes as he relentlessly perfected his technique. Obviously he didn't give a hoot what the other bowlers around him thought, either.

That determination has paid off to the tune of $1.5 million in prize money over the years. So I'm sure he can afford to bowl for real anytime, anywhere he wants.

But I wonder. Do you think he ever throws a few, *sans* ball, like the old days?

I wouldn't bet on it. But you *can* bet on this: *If shadow bowling worked for Earl, it certainly can work for you!*

READY FREDDY

OK! You're dressed to bowl. You stride into your neighborhood alley, find the front desk and rent a lane. You ask for a size ten pair of bowling shoes to rent and they give you a triple-toned, size eleven with two broken laces. They ask for one of your shoes so's that you don't walk off with the nifty footwear, and off you go with one-shoe-on and one-shoe-off to locate lane #34.

There it is!

You unload your stuff, put on the cool shoes and begin your search for the perfect house ball.

There they are!

Immediately behind all the lanes is an endless variety of balls with teeny-weeny finger holes and gaping thumb holes. After some searching you find one with a perfect fit but it weighs only 8 pounds. Finally you settle for a ball that has the right heft, but your fingers sorta swim around in the grip.

Back at your lane you set the ball in the tray behind the ball return and check the soles of your bowling shoes for any gunk that you may have picked up. Then you check out the approach area for spills or smudges.

Of course you want to set up the scoring apparatus, because even if you're by yourself you want to see how you stack up. (It's practically pointless to tell anyone starting out that scoring should be the last thing on your mind.)

The instructions for the scoreboard are only mildly confusing, and *voila!*, up flashes the scorecard on your overhead monitor and you're ready to go.

POINT OF ORIGIN

I love this term. Makes me think of the *Beginning of Man*. Or *2001: A Space Odyssey*.

This is really just a high-falutin' name for starting point. Without the ball in your hands, go over to the foul line just in front of the lane. Don't step over the line into the lane as it's extremely slick from the dressing. Next to the foul line are seven dots. Turn around at the middle dot and pace 4 1/2 steps back down the approach. There you should be in the vicinity of another identical line of seven dots. It's OK if you're not right on top of them. They're only reference points.

Make a note of where you ended up. Line up with the middle dot and some point of reference on the ball return. This should be close to your starting point.

To check it out, turn around and do the four-step boogie you've been practicing. Your sliding foot should stop a few inches in back of the foul line. You don't wanna be sliding over it onto the lane.

If it checks out, you've *almost* got your starting point.

Again, without the ball, find your *almost* starting point and face the pins. Look down at the reference dots in your vicinity. Line up the center dot with the instep of

1) Finding Your Point of Origin- Begin by placing yourself a few inches shy of the foul line at the middle dot and middle board.

2) From the foul line pace four and one-half steps following the middle board.

3) Look down and make a mental note of this spot. Line it up with any nearby dots and/or the ball return. This is your starting point. *Remember it!*

4) Standing on your spot-- If you are righthanded, place the instep of your left foot on your spot on the middle board. Place your right foot alongside about five inches back. (By the way, nice shoes!)

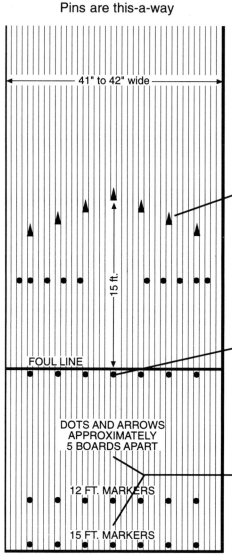

Pins are this-a-way

41" to 42" wide

15 ft.

FOUL LINE

DOTS AND ARROWS
APPROXIMATELY
5 BOARDS APART

12 FT. MARKERS

15 FT. MARKERS

This is another overhead view showing the bowler's end of an alley.

The Almighty Second Arrow-- This is your target if you're a righty. Leftys use the second arrow on the other side.

Middle Dot and Middle Board-- This is where you begin your search for a point of origin or starting point.

Point of Origin-- Your starting point will be somewhere around here on the middle board. Use the dots to line yourself up.

your left foot. If you are lefthanded, line up the center dot with the instep of your right foot. (As we continue, reverse the instructions for right and left if you are lefthanded. The following instructions will be for righthanded bowlers.)

OK. We've just fine-tuned your starting point. **This is your spot. Your point of origin for now. Remember it.**

AIMING FOR ARROWS

Now look up.

Down the alley you'll see a flying **V** of arrows about 15 feet from the foul line. Those are your spotters. **Bowlers use those arrows to aim their shots.** Those arrows are lined up exactly with the pins. As a rule, bowlers do not aim for the pins because they're so far away. The pins also shimmer in the bright lights further decreasing their desirability as a target.

Your target, your mission, is to roll your ball over the second arrow from the right, after perfectly executing the four-step boogie with a handshake. *(Holy Cow!)*

OK. BUT HOW COME THE SECOND ARROW?

The second arrow is the gateway to the strike pocket for most righthanders. Maybe a little to the right or left, but by and large, and from here to eternity, this is your aiming spot (unless you're a backup bowler, but that we'll deal with later). You will change your point of origin (maybe), but never (well, almost never) your second-arrow-aiming-spot for full-rack throws.

ROLLIN' FOR REAL

This is it! Time for the real thing.

Go over to the tray and find your ball. Pick the ball up top and bottom with both hands so there's no danger of smashed fingers. (Don't yank it up with just your fingers/thumb in the holes, either. It's too much of a strain.) Cradle it in the crook of your left arm and head back to your starting point.

Get into your stance. Eyeball that second arrow and commence the four-step approach. **As you push the ball forward and take that first step, let the ball work for you. Let it swing itself and your arm down, back, and finally forward. There's no need to force it!**

Try to *carry-the-suitcase* like you did when you shadow bowled. Forearm, wrist, and fingers are held firm and straight as the pendulum swings towards the release.

Release the ball as it passes your sliding left foot. Remember to follow-through towards your target arrow.

IT JUST DOESN'T MATTER!

In the first *Meatballs* movie with Bill Murray, there's a scene that drives home a certain message that's very appropriate at this stage in your bowling development.

In this scene, Bill Murray is addressing a cabin-full of summer campers the night before a big day of competition with a rival camp across the lake. Bill's campers are uneasy about the prospects because the other guys have always whipped them before. To a man (and woman) they are feeling defeated already.

Well, Bill gives them a pep talk about *doing the very best they can! Just give it all you got!* That sorta thing.

And then he starts chanting, *"It just doesn't matter! It just doesn't matter!,"* until the entire crew is laughing and chanting along, and their pre-game blues are all but forgotten.

The point:

No matter where that first ball ended up, no matter how many pins were knocked down, no matter what you did at this stage of the game...

Four-Step Approach (below, left to right)-- Every sport has its fundamentals. Learn them well and *then* you can develop your own game, whatever the game. The four-step is about as basic as it gets in bowling.

Set-Up...   First Step...   Second Step...

The ball is held in line with the right shoulder. The elbow is tucked in.

The right foot takes a step as the ball is pushed out.

The ball and arm begin the pendulum swing.

Third step...   Fourth Step...   Follow-Through

The ball reaches its apex in the backswing and the left arm extends for balance.

The ball and the left foot arrive at the foul line simultaneously.

The arm follows up and through the target.

Four-Step Approach (below, left to right) -- Coming at you. The approach is an athletic feat to gain timing and control. More specifically, it spreads the work of propelling the ball from your hand and arm, to your back and legs.

Set-Up...   *First Step...*   *Second Step...*

Check out the look in Jim's eyes. Obviously he's focused on his target. You can almost see the mental bridge connecting his mind and body to his arrow 15 feet down the lane.

Third step...   *Fourth Step...*   *Follow-Through*

Note the arm swing in all these pix. Exactly like a pendulum swinging in a perfect arc at right angles to the shoulders.

Four-Step Approach (below, left to right)-- From another angle. Although for the sake of instruction the various stages of the four-step are broken down into these sequences, it's important to remember that the real thing is a smooth, flowing movement.

Set-Up...   *First Step...*   *Second Step...*

Debbie is glued to her target from start to finish. She steps straight ahead and pushes the ball out directly from her right shoulder to the target arrow.

Third step...   *Fourth Step...*   *Follow-Through*

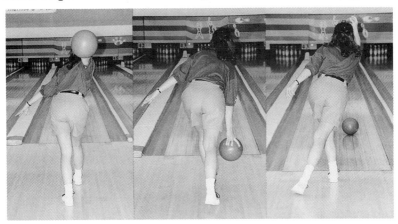

Note the arc of the ball as it swings. Always true to the target line. It's not sheer muscle power that enables her to achieve this swing. It's the proper pushaway and the four steps that really propel the ball.

Perfect Form-- Nothing shows off the grace of good bowling fundamentals like the properly executed follow-through.

It just doesn't matter!

Don't worry about your score for now. Don't worry about getting a strike. Don't be embarrassed when you pitch into the ditch.

You're working on fundamentals. You're getting a *feel* for the mechanics. You're trying to establish a *rhythm*. These things take time and practice.

Hey! You'll get it soon enough!

OVERVIEW

1) **Once you've found your point of origin, stick with it for several frames** until you get to know how you throw the ball. You'll make adjustments later.

2) Each time before you bowl, make a concerted effort to relax and focus on the job at hand. **Concentrate!**

3) **Get set in your stance: Line the ball up with your right shoulder. Hold that wrist firm and straight. Your right elbow is close to your side. Square your shoulders to the lane.**

4) **Eyeball that second arrow** until you burn a hole there.

5) As you move your right foot, push your ball forward towards the target arrow. Chant this: **Move foot, move ball! Move foot, move ball!**

6) **Let the ball do the work! Make like a pendulum. Keep the arm swing straight.**

7) **Ball and sliding left foot should arrive at the foul line at the same time.** That's how ya know if you're doing the dance right.

8) **Release the ball with a handshake.** Like you're tossing a suitcase.

9) **Follow-through with your throwing arm.** Straight through the target line.

10) You may tear your eyes off the target arrow **only after the ball has rolled passed it.**

It's a jumble of things to do and remember for now, but with a few throws you'll begin to develop a groove. It just takes awhile to get used to the ball, the way it swings, and the way it comes off your hand. Before long the pieces will come together and you'll be able to *feel* how it's done.

What's Your **Ball** **Doing?**

PATHFINDING

After you have bowled for awhile, you will settle into a way of setting-up and delivering the ball. You will have discovered a groove for yourself. Consequently the path of your ball will begin to settle into a pattern as well. And that path will reveal just what kind of bowler you have become so far.

HOOK

Developing a simple *hook* is not as contrived as most folks think. In fact, if you set-up and deliver the ball as instructed in these pages, you will throw a ball that rolls straight for about 30-40 feet and then curves, or hooks to the left if you are a righthanded bowler.

What causes the hooking action is the handshake release. When the ball leaves the hand in a handshake, the thumb is at a 10 o'clock position and the fingers at a 4 and 5 o'clock position. The thumb naturally leaves the ball first (it's shorter!) leaving just the fingers. For a nano second, the fingers lift the ball on its right side and give the ball a counter-clockwise spin. The ball skids and scoots along in a straight path for awhile until the finger-spin grabs hold of the lane and makes the ball hook left.

The hook is the most recommended type of shot to deliver.

When aimed correctly, the hook is the most effective way to spill pins. **It comes into the 1-3 pocket at the ideal angle to hit the key pins in the rack, which in turn scatter all the rest.** Its spinning action prevents it from being easily deflected on its path of destruction and really works the rack in general.

When you see the pros bowl, they all utilize some sort of hook. Of course, their versions are oft times so exaggerated and embellished by wrist and arm movements that they look very difficult to emulate. And they are for most bowlers. But the simple hook is well within reach.

Who knows. Maybe you'll get it right off!

STRAIGHT BALL

With no instruction at all, most folks throw a *straight ball*. As the ball leaves the hand, the thumb is straight up in a 12 o'clock position and the fingers are directly underneath the ball. This release imparts no spin. The ball goes pretty much where it's pointed in a straight line.

It's easier to throw the ball this way because it feels more natural and more secure than the suitcase/handshake release.

There's nothing wrong with throwing a straight ball. Heck, there's nothing wrong with throwing anything if you're having a good time. It's just that **the straight ball isn't quite as effective as the hook because it doesn't enter the pocket at an ideal angle and**

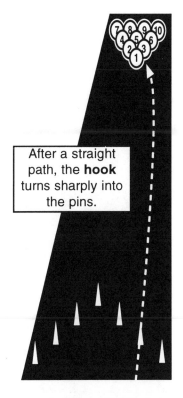

After a straight path, the **hook** turns sharply into the pins.

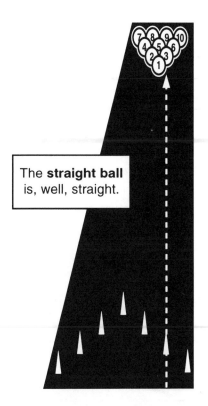

The **straight ball** is, well, straight.

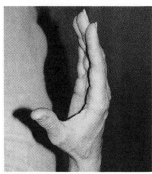

Hook Ball Release-
The fingers give the ball a lift and a counter-clockwise spin as the ball leaves the hand.

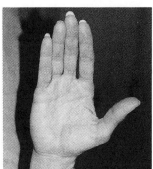

Straight Ball Release--
No spin is imparted as the ball is rolled straight off the palm and fingers.

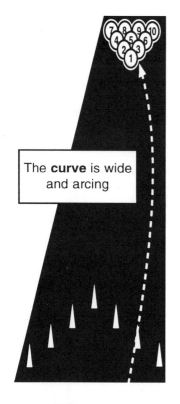

The **curve** is wide and arcing

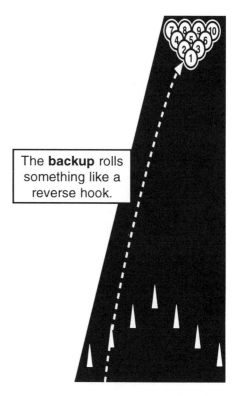

The **backup** rolls something like a reverse hook.

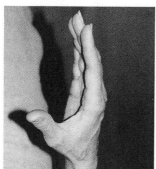

Curve Ball-- Like the hook, the bowler uses a handshake release but adds extra lift and/or action to the ball.

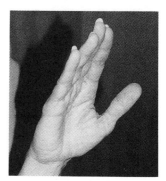

Backup Ball--The ball rolls off the thumb-side of the hand and imparts a clockwise spin to the ball.

70

because it doesn't have any spin. Without spin the ball is more easily deflected by the pins.

BACKUP BALL

This is like a reverse hook. The ball is released with the thumb way over towards 1 or 2 o'clock. The fingers end up giving the ball a clockwise spin that causes it to curve to the right.

With some adjusting, a dedicated backup bowler can make this work. *Not recommended.*

CURVE BALL

This is an exaggerated hook. The ball is released with the thumb towards 9 o'clock and an extra lift of the fingers. This imparts mucho spin on the ball that results in a super hook that's very hard to control.

It can also work. *Not recommended.*

SO, WHAT ARE YOU?

If you have been bowling with any degree of consistency for awhile, one of these shots fits you. You can adjust aspects of your game to fit your shot, or you can try to change the way you shoot.

Although the hook is the favored shot, no one is going to take issue with you if you score well with a straight ball, or a backup ball or a curve ball. Knocking down pins is the name of the game. **If you have a style that CONSISTENTLY works for you, stick with it!**

ADJUSTMENTS

Hook

If you're missing the 1-3 pocket to the left, move your point of origin to the left. If you're missing the 1-3 pocket to the right, move your point of origin to the right. Keep the second arrow from the right as your target.

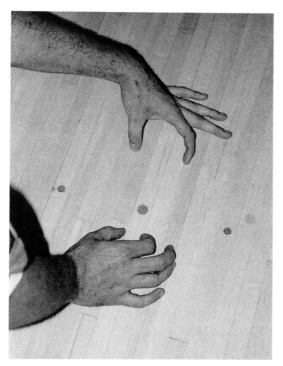

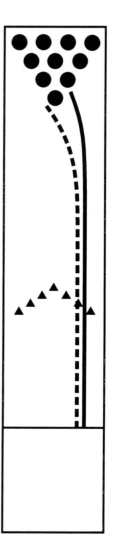

As a rule, if you make a one board adjustment to the right or left of your starting point, the ball will make a three board adjustment by the time it reaches the pins.

This system only works, however, if your shots are *consistent*. And **that** is the key!

Be sure to make your adjustments bit by bit. You'll find a little will go a long way. By moving ONE board width (referring to the one inch boards that comprise a lane), you will change the impact point at the pins by THREE board widths.

Straight Ball

If it's a straight ball that you throw, your point of origin should move one dot right from center. Continue to use the second arrow as a target. This will give you maximum angle into the pocket. *Again, adjust in the direction of your error:* adjust left for wide-left and right for wide-right.

Backup Ball

Use the first dot to the right of center as a point of origin. Use the third arrow from the right as a target. Adjust left for wide-left and right for wide-right.

Curve Ball

Use the same procedure as with the hook shot.

DO IT YOUR WAY THE SAME WAY

Roseanne is a lousy bowler. She doesn't even *like* to bowl in the first place, but her sister and their mutual friends do. So she goes along just to be part of the crowd. She could care less how she performs, and it shows. Especially when she lets loose with the ball.

Without even looking down the alley, she lofts the ball up and lets it crash into the boards. Without a backward glance, she returns to friends, food, and holding court as usual. Which, of course, are her main interests anyway.

On the other hand, if you watch the pros on TV, you'll witness an entirely different approach to the game. My goodness! The way they can make that ball *work!* They all have a twirly-whirly delivery that sends their balls spinning and careening down the lane to demolish the racks of pins almost every single time! They make it look so easy, but you know it can't be. No way!

At this point, you realize that you don't bowl like they do on TV. Maybe you started out like *Rosy*, but you're alot better now. You'd *like* to bowl like the pros, but how do they do all that fancy wrist movement? How do they control it?

The thing is, you're looking at the very best. And like the pros in any sport, they've got mega hours of time invested in their sport. More than most of us will ever dream of investing. You can definitely learn from watching certain aspects of their game, but some stuff, especially the release, will be impossible for you to emulate from just watching TV. That takes years of practice and instruction.

What you can do is improve on *your* game. Build on the fundamentals and make adjustments as you improve. Make sure you at least *try* to develop a hook shot. Whatever you end up with, work on *consistency*. *Know your shot. Get it down so that it goes the same place every time.*

Without consistency you cannot successfully adjust for your spare shots or different lane conditions. What good is moving one board left, to hit a spot three boards over, if your shots are all over the map to begin with?

You ain't *Rosy* (there's only one).

You ain't a pro (just yet!).

But you've got *your* shot. Work out the bugs. Make it roll the *same* way *each* time...

And watch dem pins tumble!

WADDYA MEAN YOU DIDN'T KNOCK DOWN ALL THE PINS WITH YOUR FIRST THROW!

For those of you who aren't throwing strikes all the time, you gotta learn how to knock down what's left of the rack with your second toss. Making spares is right up there with making strikes. Actually, it's pretty much half your game. Making spares ain't as sexy as strikes, but without them your scores will not improve.

So buck up! Nobody throws strikes all the time. Shake it off and find your focus. You'll need it to finish the job.

MAJOR POINTS

1) **Set-up on the side of the approach opposite to the location of the spare pin or spare group.** If the remaining pin(s) are on the right, move your starting point to the left. Spares left, move right. This positioning gives the bowler more lane to work with.

Set-up on the side of the lane opposite to your spare group. This will give you more lane to make your shot.

2) Make sure you hit the pin closest to you.

3) Aim your ball so that it directly hits as many pins as possible.

4) Square your shoulders to the target.

5) In seeking the ideal angle, remember that a one board adjustment at the start, or point of origin, will result in a three board adjustment at the finish, or point of impact.

SPARE (ME THE) SCIENCE

I deliberately left out what are actually called the *Scientific Spare Systems.* These are proven methods of adjusting for all the various spare combos for both right- and lefthanded bowlers. As you become more seasoned you'll want to study them. But the scope of this book falls far short of anything scientific, thank you very much. We don't wanna mix the wiring between the right and left sides of your brain any more than we already have!

SPARE TRIVIA

– There are 1,023 possible spare leaves (pins left standing).

– The target area for a single pin is 21.95 inches. Your ball is 8.59 inches wide and a pin is 4.76 inches wide. Since you can convert the single pin from either side, multiply the ball's width twice and add the pin width.

– Pins left standing that are side-to-side as you see them from the approach are called fit splits. They are 7.2344 inches apart and a ball that is aimed between them will topple both.

– Every time you miss a spare, you lose at least 10 points from your final score.

WHAT'S YOUR ANGLE?

Here are the left, right, and middle spare leaves with

charts depicting the ideal angles to convert. The starting points indicated are a good place for you to begin, but should be adjusted according to your shot.

The following charts show the various spare groups and the suggested shot for each.

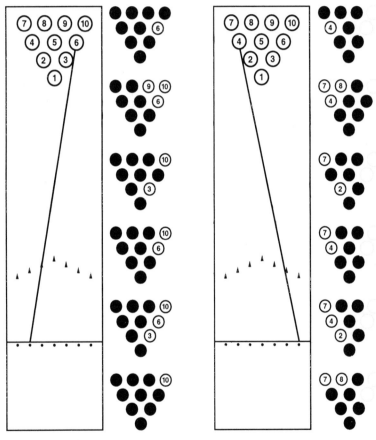

Right Side Spares   **Left Side Spares**

Remember: For each board width you move at the start, or point of origin, the ball's impact point at the pins will move three boards. **If the ball veers too much to the right, adjust to the right of your point of origin. Wide-left, adjust left.**

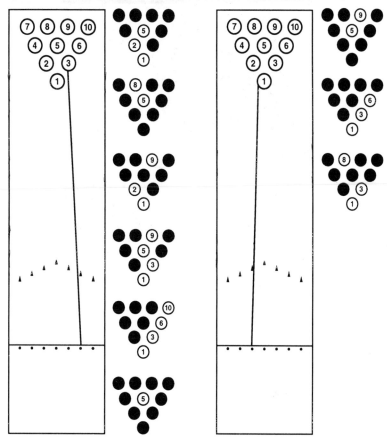

Strike Ball Spares   **Middle Spares**

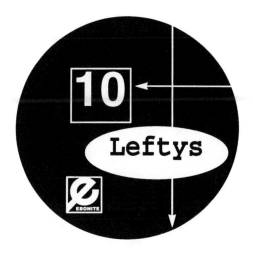

After nine chapters of righthanded instruction, here's a treat for the southpaws. And it's *because* you're such a minority that it happens to be such good news...

OFF THE BEATEN TRACK

The right side of any given lane is literally rutted by all the righthanded hurlers. Not that you can see, but the tracks of a zillion balls are there. Making it almost impossible to successfully throw well aimed balls into the pocket over the first arrow. The ball hits the ruts and gets deflected. Hence the route over the second arrow. Along with everyone else.

It would be nice to throw over that first arrow because a good hook can enter the 1-3 pocket at a much better angle to upset the pins. The greater angle means the ball will meet with less deflection, thus driving down more pins.

But you leftys don't have that problem. Fewer leftys, fewer tracks.

The Leftfield Advantage:

1) You are blessed with a **better playing field** that,

2) enables you to throw a **higher percentage strike ball,**

3) demands **fewer adjustments,**

4) thereby enabling you to **concentrate on one basic set-up and stroke,** and

5) thereby enabling you to be **more consistent** than the entire righty bowler population.

Is this a beautiful sport or what? The world's most maligned group is avenged each and every day in bowling centers across the globe. And it never took an act of Congress!

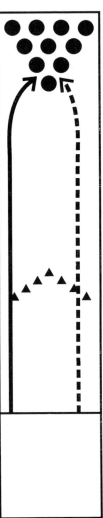

The lefthander's track over the first arrow from the left boasts a greater angle into the strike pocket than that of the righthander over the second arrow from the right.

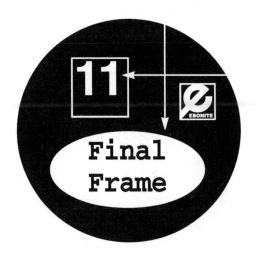

TROUBLE SHOOTING

Don't think of your delivery in terms of parts.

From set-up to follow-through your delivery is one continuous, flowing thing. When you're doing it right, it *feels* **right.**

If stuff is going haywire, go back to the fundamentals. Practice your shadow bowling again to regain timing and rhythm. Like a dance step. Go over those basic instructions in chapters six and seven and reapply them until they work for you.

Have someone watch you who is at least at your level and whom you feel comfortable listening to. **A real coach** *who knows* **is best. As previously stated, real-live, competent instruction is priceless.** The problem might seem to be insurmountable, but oft times a simple adjustment can put you and your wandering ball back on track.

Common Faults:

***Roundhouse Swing*--**The ball has not been drawn back straight from the target. Probably because the ball was set-up too far in front of the body instead of in-line with the throwing shoulder.

***Outside Swing*--** Again, the arm is not swinging at a right angle to the body. This time because the ball was probably set-up too far to the bowler's right.

***Dropped Shoulder*--** The shoulder has dropped too much during the final step of the approach. The ball has dropped to the lane before the release.

Common Faults:

High and Centered Set-Up-- Setting-up too high will give you too much speed in your backswing. Also, setting-up mid-body will result in a roundhouse swing.

Low and Centered Set-Up- Setting-up too low will severely impair your approach. Again, the ball should be held in-line with the throwing shoulder.

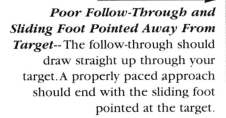

Poor Follow-Through and Sliding Foot Pointed Away From Target-- The follow-through should draw straight up through your target. A properly paced approach should end with the sliding foot pointed at the target.

I WAS DOING GREAT `TIL I MET YOU!

Learning the game is sometimes like building a house on a bad foundation. You get to a certain point only to realize that you have to tear it all back down to the weakness in the structure in order build it back up again the way you intended.

It's easy to fall into little ruts of style that work up to a point, but prevent you from getting any better. That's why you should get instruction before all your little habits become too ingrained. The longer you bowl with a problem, the longer and harder it is too overcome.

When I first bowled, I couldn't wait to unleash the ball. I don't think I took two steps during my approach. And I did pretty good. Or so I thought until I had my first lesson. As a matter of fact, I bowled a 175, my highest game ever up to that point, no more than ten minutes before that darn lesson. Of course, my shoulder throbbed and my balance was non-existent, but hey, scoreboard baby!

Well, my instructor checked me out for a few frames and was not at all impressed. He said I couldn't go on muscling the ball and expect to really improve. He had me learn the four-step approach.

It was *hard!* I was all screwed up trying to time my pushaway with my first step. And those four steps felt like forty after my two-step approach. Every one of my balls went into the gutter. *What was this guy doing to my game!*

But in time I got it. The four-step eased the strain on my arm and shoulder, and put it on my back where it belongs. It helped my rhythm and I began to develop balance.

My game got torn down, all right, but only to create a better foundation for progress. And that's how it goes as you try to reach different levels. You'll slump before you surge.

So try not to be a crybaby when your instructor tells you to try something new. It just might be good advice. And don't wait too long to ask for it in the first place.

MIXING IT UP AND BOWLING BETTER

It's easy to join a league. Most bowling centers fall all over themselves to entice newcomers. There aren't any tryouts. You'll bowl with folks at your level.

It's fun to join a league. It ain't like making friends at a new surf spot. Everybody wants you there!

Playing in leagues is a great way to keep bowling and get better. The friendly competition pushes you to concentrate on your game, and the schedule makes you play.

Besides, staying at home and watching TV will rot your brain. Just like Mom said. *And that goes for video games, too!*

Final Frame

Bowlers
TimeLine

Make no mistake, bowling is as old as the hills.

When the pharaohs weren't building pyramids, they were rollin' rocks. In this country, bowling came to prominence right around the time Abner Doubleday's little game began to draw crowds and enthusiasts.

And the personalities! *Martin Luther. Sir Francis Drake. Abe Lincoln. Ralph Cramden.* That's some bowling team they have upstairs.

Here's a very quick trip through *Bowler Time*:

5200 BC-- Well-to-do Egyptians enjoy a bowling-like game by tossing round stones at rock pins. Upon death, the stones and pins were buried along with them in order to maintain averages in the hereafter.

A little later in the South Pacific-- In-between long outrigger rides and surf sessions, Polynesians develop the game of *Ula Maika*. A knock `em down game that required the bowler to make a 60 foot throw to the target. This, of course, is the same distance that modern bowlers must negotiate today.

When in Rome-- Ancient Roman artifacts indicate an early Italian strain of bowling.

4 AD-- Roving Germanic barbarians take time out to throw a few and invent a type of bowling called *kegeling.*

1505-- **Martin Luther** builds his own lane in order to play *ninepins.* This particular game sweeps throughout Europe and is the version of bowling that first comes to America 150 years later.

Meanwhile in England-- *Skittles* is all the rage.

1588-- Perhaps the most confident underdog in history, **Sir Francis Drake** delays his very historic battle with the Spanish Armada in order to finish his game of ninepins. Afterward, feeling loose and relaxed, he sets sail and snuffs the invading fleet. His score that day is unknown.

1646-- America joins the bandwagon when a Knickerbocker bowls the first stateside frame ever in New York City.

1732-- A parade ground at Battery Fort in NYC is converted to a bowling area and deemed Bowling Green. This is still the name of that piece of real estate located on lower Broadway.

1818-- Bowling makes its American literary debut in *Rip Van Winkle* by **Washington Irving.**

Early-Mid 1800s-- Bowling takes root in New York, Syracuse, Buffalo, Cincinnati, Chicago and Milwaukee. All locations with large German populations.

– Bowling is an outdoor sport until 1840.

– In NYC, bowling becomes a huge fad with alleys reported on almost every block.

– **Abe Lincoln** relaxes from rail splitting by bowling in Illinois for high average.

– Bowling continues its booming growth but is

plagued by localism, rowdyism, and gambling. Much like its sporting peer, baseball.

1841-- Connecticut outlaws ninepins due to the influence of gambling rackets and rowdyism.

– A tenth pin is added somewhere along the line.

1875-- The **National Bowling Congress (NBC)** is formed in NYC by delegates from nine local clubs. This is bowling's first major attempt to organize.

1895-- The **American Bowling Congress (ABC)** is born in NYC. Standardization truly begins. The game is fundamentally the same today.

1916-- Here come the ladies! The **Women's International Bowling Congress (WIBC)** is created in St. Louis.

1936-- Organized bowling for young people begins in Chicago by the formation of a city-wide intramural league.

1946-- The American Junior Bowling Congress is founded.

1952-- More than any other single invention, the automatic pinsetter revolutionizes the game and puts thousands of teenage boys out of a job. This single invention helps bowling become absolutely gigantic.

Other improvements come fast and furious:

– Automatic scoring devices.

– Scoring projection units.

– Automatic foul detectors.

– Under-the-floor ball return channels.

– Automatic hand dryers.

– The Bowling Center Era begins. Bowling sheds its somewhat unsavory image and becomes a family recreation. Large, fully-automated, sparkling clean and attractive, bowling centers replace the small, dank, and creaky alleys of old.

1961-- The ABC joins the Federation Internationale

des Quilleurs, bowling's international ruling body.

1963-- The Youth Bowling Association is formed by the Bowling Proprietors of America.

– The ABC creates the first Seniors program.

1966-- The ABC creates a Collegiate Division.

1975-- The ABC/WIBC Collegiate Division is founded.

1982-- The **Young American Bowling Alliance (YABA)** is created by combining the American Junior Bowling Congress, the Youth Bowling Association, and the ABC/WIBC Collegiate Division.

1983-- The WIBC Championship tournament in La Vegas attracts 14,430 five-women teams, the biggest team entry in history, and 75,480 individuals, a world record. The WIBC has become the largest sports organization for women in the world.

1986-- The TEAM USA program selects WIBC/ABC members to compete in world-wide tournament play and ultimately in the Olympic Games.

1988-- Bowling takes part in the Olympic Games in Seoul, South Korea as an exhibition sport.

1991-- Bowling becomes a medal sport in the Pan American Games in Cuba. Fidel Castro presents gold medals to US bowlers.

1992-- The ABC introduces the National Team Challenge, an attempt to bring team bowling back to the forefront. It is so successful it becomes the World Team Challenge the next year.

1995-- The ABC Tournament in Reno, Nevada opens the National Bowling Stadium with a record 17,285 five-player teams and 92,000 individuals, a world record.

1995-- The ABC celebrates its Centennial on September 9.

Glossary

Action-- The movement applied to the ball upon release.

Alley-- A bowling lane or bowling center. An older reference.

Angle-- Refers to the path of the bowling ball as it approaches the pins.

Approach-- That area before the foul line. This is the bowler's runway.

Arrows-- The pointed guides imbedded in the lane about 15 feet out from the foul line. Used by bowlers to line-up their shots.

Backup Ball-- Type of shot with a clockwise spin (righthanded bowlers). Ball is released with the thumb in a one or two o'clock position.

Backswing-- That part of the delivery sequence where the arm and ball swing to an apex behind the bowler.

Boards-- Refers to the boards that run the length of a bowling lane.

Channel-- Refers to the gutter located on either side of the bowling lane.

Conditioner-- The oil or dressing applied to the

lanes.

Conventional Grip-- The type of grip on a ball where the fingers are inserted fully to the second knuckle.

Converting the Spare-- Knocking down the remaining pins on a bowler's second throw.

Curve Ball-- Type of shot that travels in a wide, sweeping arc due to an exaggerated counter-clockwise spin (righthanded bowlers).

Deflection-- Movement of the ball from its true path caused by the pins.

Dressing-- Refers to the oil or conditioner that is applied to the lanes.

Dumping the ball-- Dropping the ball at the foul line before release.

Error-- Missing a spare other than a split.

Fit Splits-- Type of split in which pins are left standing side-by-side.

Foul-- Touching or going over the foul line when delivering the ball.

Foul Line--The line separating the approach from the lane or alley.

Four-Step Approach-- A delivery that utilizes four steps. The most recommended approach.

Frame-- Games are divided into ten such units. Something like an inning is to baseball.

Grip-- The *handle* of a bowling ball. Includes holes for the thumb and the two middle fingers.

Gutter-- The drop-off channel located on either side of the lane.

Gutter Ball-- Ball which rolls into the gutter.

Headpin--The lead pin in a rack of pins. The #1 pin.

Hook Ball--Type of shot that breaks sharply into the pins.

Hooking Lane-- Type of lane that allows good hooking action.

Holding Lane-- Type of lane that does not allow much action on the ball.

Kegeling-- Old German form of bowling.

Lane-- The 60 foot-long area from foul line to pins. The alley.

Leave-- The pins left standing after the first throw.

Lofting-- Tossing the ball in the air upon delivery.

Miss-- Failure to convert a spare other than a split. An error.

Ninepins-- The ancestor of tenpins or modern bowling. Developed in Europe and transported to America in the 1600s.

Perfect Game--A 300 score.

Pin Action-- Movement of the pins after the ball has struck.

Pocket-- The strike target area on a full rack of pins. The area between the 1-3 pins for a righthander, and the area between the 1-2 pins for a lefty.

Point of Origin-- The starting point in a bowler's approach.

Pushaway-- That part of the delivery sequence where the ball is pushed out with the first step.

Release-- That part of the delivery sequence where the thumb and fingers impart any action to the ball and come out of the ball.

Return-- The rails upon which balls return to the bowler. Also the rack where they return to rest.

Set-up-- The stance a bowler takes to initiate an approach.

Settee-- Sitting area at the base of the approach.

Shadow Bowling-- Practicing the delivery without a bowling ball.

Span-- The distance between thumb and finger holes on a bowling ball.

Spare Systems-- Scientific methods to effectively aim for and knock down the pins left standing after the first throw.

Spare-- Knocking down all ten pins in two trys.

Split-- Refers to any combination of pins left standing after the first delivery where the pin(s) in between and /or immediately in front are knocked down. The headpin must also be knocked down.

Straight Ball-- Type of shot that has no spin or action. Rolls in a straight line.

Strike-- Knocking down all the pins with the first ball.

Track-- The invisible rut created by numerous balls traveling over the same path.

Resources

BOWLING CENTERS

The epicenter for all bowling activity will always be down at the alley. The centers usually have it all:

- *Instruction*
- *Leagues*
- *Contests*
- *Pro Shops* where you can buy balls, bags, shoes, and clothing. And get your ball drilled, or patched and redrilled, or repaired.
- *Literature & Videos* for free and/or for sale.
- *Information* about organizations, bowling camps, and national contests.
- *Bowlers* to talk to.
- *A place to bowl!*

Every community has a town hall, a police station, a fire house, and a bowling center. I know it's written somewhere. It's more or less unAmerican for a town *not* to have a bowling center. Just look in the yellow pages.

BOWLING MAGAZINES

Bowling Digest
990 Grove St.
Evanston, IL 60201
708-491-6440

Bowling Highlights News
131 Winthrop Ave.
Liberty, NY 12754
914-292-9114

Bowling Industry
660 Hampshire Rd.
#200
Westlake Village, CA 91361
818-879-9986

Bowlers Journal
200 South Michigan Ave.
Suite 1430
Chicago, IL 60604
312-266-7171

Bowling Magazine
(Official Publication of the *American Bowling Congress*)
5301 South 76th Street
Greendale, Wis. 53129
414-421-6400

Bowling This Month
PO Box 35847
Houston, TX 77235
713-729-7344

TELEVISION

Check your listings for championship events. Every week there's something!

BOOKS & VIDEOS

Check out your local bowling center and library, of course, but *the source for all bowling knowledge is:*

Bowler's Bookstore
Tech-Ed publishing Company
PO Box 4
Deerfield, IL 60015
708-945-3169
800-521-BOWL

Call `em up and ask for their catalog. Over 50 books and videos about all aspects of the game. If it's in print, they've got it!

MUSEUMS

Bowling Hall of Fame and Museum
111 Stadium Plaza
St. Louis, MO 63102
314-231-6340

ORGANIZATIONS

The following organizations are very happy to provide a wealth of information about the sport and themselves:

American Bowling Congress (ABC)
Bowling Headquarters
5301 South 76th St.
Greendale, WI 53129
414-421-6400

Bowling, Inc.
2300 Claredon Blvd.
Arlington, VA 22201
703-841-1660

Bowling Proprietors Association of America (BPAA)
PO Box 5802
Arlington, TX 76011
817-649-5105

USA Bowling
Bowling Headquarters
5301 South 76th St.
Greendale, WI 53129
414-421-9008

Women's International Bowling Congress (WIBC)
Bowling Headquarters
5301 South 76th St.
Greendale, WI 53129
414-421-9000

Young American Bowling Alliance (YABA)
Bowling Headquarters
5301 South 76th St.
Greendale, WI 53129
414-421-9000

Ebonite

Bibliography

-Anthony, Earl. *Winning Bowling*. Chicago, Illinois.: Contemporary Books, Inc., 1994.

-James, Steve. *Bowlers Guide*. Greendale, Wisconsin.: American Bowling Congress, 1992.

-Semenik, Joe. *A Bowling Bible*.

-Strickland, Robert H. *Bowling: Steps to Success*. Champaign, Illinois.: Leisure Press, 1989.

-Taylor, Dawson. *Mastering Bowling*. Chicago, Illinois.: Contemporary Books, Inc., 1980.

-Weiskopf, Herm. *Bowling: Styling Your Game for Success*. New York, New York.: Time, Inc., 1987.

-Wene, Sylvia. *The Women's Bowling Guide*. New York, New York.: D. Mckay Co., 1959

Index

American Bowling Congress 25,91
Adjustments 71-73
Aiming (use of arrows) 58-59
Anthony, Earl 53-54

Bush, George 14
Backup ball 70-71
Balls
    fitting 20, 23
    specs 25
Bowling
    basic fundamentals 55-66
    how played 25-34
    stats 14
Carter, Jimmy 14
Clinton, Bill 14-15
Clothing 18-20
    shoes 19-20
Common faults 84-85
Conditioning of lanes 26, 33
Courtesy 40-44
Curve ball 70-71

Drake, Sir Francis 15, 89, 90

Federation Internationale des Quilleurs 14, 91
Follow-through 48-51, 61-65
Four-step approach 48-51, 60-63, 65

Grip (conventional) 20-21, 23
Gear 18-24

History (of bowling) 89-93
Hook ball 67-69
Hoover, Herbert 14

Instruction 16, 83, 86-87
Irving, Washington 90

Kegeling 90

Lanes 25-27, 32, 58
Lincoln, Abe 14, 15, 89-90
Lofting 40, 41
Lefty bowling 81-82
Luther, Martin 89, 90

Meatballs (the movie) 60
Murray, Bill 60

National Bowling Congress 91
National Team Challenge 92
Nixon, Richard 14, 15

Olympics 92

Pan American Games 92
Pins 26-27
Pocket 28-29, 68, 81-82
Point of origin 56-58

Release (hand position) 52-53, 65, 67-68
Right-of-way 42, 44
Roseanne 73-74

Safety 45-46

Scientific spare system 77
Scoring 34-39
Setting-up 48-51, 61-63, 65
Shadow Bowling 47-54
Shoes 19-20
Skittles 90
Spares 29, 75-80
Spare groups 78-79
Straight Ball 68-69, 71
Strike 28

Trouble shooting 83-87
Trumen, Harry 14

Ula Maika 89-90

Women's International Bowling Congress 25, 91
Wrist brace 22-23

Young American Bowling Alliance 92

About the Author

Doug Werner is the creator/author of the highly acclaimed *Start-Up Sports Series*. His books include *Surfer's Start-Up, Snowboarder's Start-Up, Sailor's Start-Up, In-Line Skater's Start-Up* and now, *Bowler's Start-Up*. The no-frills, fun-to-read, fun-to-learn instructional series is endorsed by leading publications, manufacturers, organizations, athletes, and coaches in the sporting world. A graduate of Cal State Long Beach, he also owns and operates a graphics business in San Diego, California.

The New Ebonite Omega with Cast Acryllium Cover.

DOWN THE LANE, IT'S A DREAM.
THROUGH THE POCKET, IT'S A MANIAC.

Moving ball technology to the next level is no drive in the park. But the new Ebonite Omega makes that leap. And you're going to love the ride.

The new Cast Acryllium Cover (CAC), together with patented, Level 4 Core Technology, gives your game the ultimate in pocket-tracking control and pin-crushing power.

It literally repels oil and unleashes an explosive force of energy into the pins.

Plus, the durability of CAC gives Omega a level of resistance to nicks, chipping and track marks that no reactive ball can match.

So ask your pro today about the new Ebonite Omega. Nothing can surpass the power of Omega.

Nothing.